Hustling and Bustling
DIGGERS

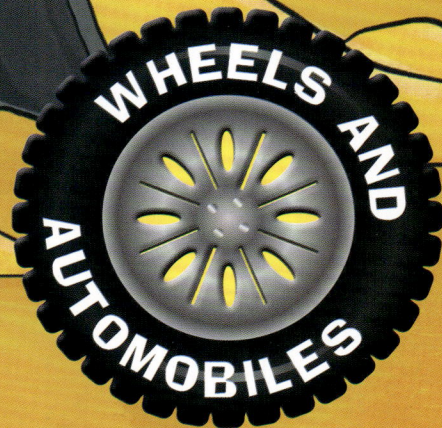

WHEELS AND AUTOMOBILES

FOX EYE
PUBLISHING

A digger is a machine that helps us to make buildings and roads.

Diggers dig deep into the ground.
They also lift heavy loads.

smashing

digging

Each digger has a different job. Some push.
Some dig. Some smash. Some haul.

hauling

How many diggers can you see in this picture?
Can you count them all?

bulldozer

tracks

The workers are on a building site.
First comes a bulldozer on tracks.

The bulldozer clears the dirt and rocks.
It makes the ground flat.

**front
loader**

A front loader lifts the dirt and
rocks into a dumper truck.

dumper truck

The dumper takes the dirt away.
Its back tips up and down slides the muck.

backhoe digger

bucket

Next, it is time to dig some holes.
Here come some backhoe diggers.

They scoop the dirt up in their buckets.
Now, it is time for a bigger digger!

excavator

rock hammer

Here comes a giant digger.
It is called an excavator.

It can dig huge holes and smash through
rock with its special rock hammer.

tracks

An excavator can do many jobs. It can lift heavy things and knock things down.

Excavators have tracks, not wheels,
to stop them sinking into the ground.

grapple —

This excavator has a grapple. A grapple is really neat!

A grapple can move heavy things around
or take a building down piece by piece.

The water pipes are all in place.
The backhoes fill the trenches with dirt.

trench

The building foundations are being laid.
The building team is getting to work.

At last, the building is going up.
What do you think it can be?

A car park, a stadium or a cinema?
What can you see?

Bustling Words

Backhoe diggers scoop up mud and rocks in their buckets.

A **bucket** is part of a digger that scoops up mud and rocks.

A **building site** is where buildings are made.

A **bulldozer** is a powerful machine that pushes away mud and rocks.

A **dumper truck** carries mud and rocks to a dumper site.

An **excavator** is a giant digger for digging large holes.

A **front loader** is a truck that lifts mud and rocks into a dumper truck.

Loads are things that are lifted up.

A **rock hammer** breaks up big rocks.

Slides means to move over something smoothly.

Smash means to break something up.

A **stadium** is a place where people watch sports.

Tracks are parts of a machine that are used instead of wheels on muddy ground. They work like wheels, to move the machine across the ground.

First published in 2024 by Fox Eye Publishing
Unit 31, Vulcan House Business Centre,
Vulcan Road, Leicester, LE5 3EF
www.foxeyepublishing.com

Author: Katherine Eason
Art director: Paul Phillips
Cover designer: Emma Bailey
Editor: Jenny Rush

All illustrations by Eszter Szepvolgyi

978-1-80445-340-7

Printed in China